T0380301

YOU DON'T KNOW *Me*

DONNA L PRINCE-BAYLIS

BALBOA
PRESS

A DIVISION OF HAY HOUSE

Balboa Press books may be ordered through booksellers or by contacting:

Balboa Press
A Division of Hay House
1663 Liberty Drive
Bloomington, IN 47403
www.balboapress.com.au
1 (877) 407-4847

Because of the dynamic nature of the Internet, any web addresses or links contained in this book may have changed since publication and may no longer be valid. The views expressed in this work are solely those of the author and do not necessarily reflect the views of the publisher, and the publisher hereby disclaims any responsibility for them.

The author of this book does not dispense medical advice or prescribe the use of any technique as a form of treatment for physical, emotional, or medical problems without the advice of a physician, either directly or indirectly. The intent of the author is only to offer information of a general nature to help you in your quest for emotional and spiritual well-being. In the event you use any of the information in this book for yourself, which is your constitutional right, the author and the publisher assume no responsibility for your actions.

Any people depicted in stock imagery provided by Thinkstock are models, and such images are being used for illustrative purposes only.
Certain stock imagery © Thinkstock.

Print information available on the last page.

ISBN: 978-1-4525-3146-5 (sc)
ISBN: 978-1-4525-3149-6 (e)

Balboa Press rev. date: 10/28/2015

Dedicated to my family and friends who accept me for me.
Who have been with me through all the highs
and lows in life and always stood by me.
Thank You.

To my children, my life, Oscar and Kalani, to remind you to
dream big, aim high and be the best that you can be.
Never let anyone or anything stand in the
way of your love, laughter and life.

Mum xoxo

CONTENTS

Preface ix

Acknowledgements xi

Introduction xiii

You Don't Know Me 1

Unbreakable 2

My First Love 3

The Hidden Me 4

To Lose, is to Win 6

Dad 7

Mum 8

Brother 10

Sister 11

Why? 14

Drawn 16

The Player 18

Bb3 19

Nan 20

Love Me, Love Me Not 22

Bb3'S 1st Birthday 23

My Promise 24

The Spark that No Longer Fires 25

Forgiveness 26

Lonely 28

My Friend 29

Lost 30

My Life 32

Fight On 34

Again 35

PREFACE

Some people hide, some seek adventure - I write.
I always have. On scrap paper, in the back cover of my text books, anywhere I could. Over the years it's been a way to celebrate, escape and even confront what's happening in my life.
I write what I feel - it's always straight from the heart.
I remember my first poem. I was in primary school and a friend and I wrote about war and peace. We would jump rope at recess reciting it. Later, in high school, a rewritten version of that poem won a writing competition and was published in the school year book.
Unfortunately it, and many others have been misplaced over time. They'd get thrown into the back of a cupboard, a drawer and eventually thrown out.
I'd never shared my writing, never felt it was good enough or that anyone else would want to read it.
Until recently.
I asked a dear friend to read some pieces. Baring my heart and soul was nerve racking, terrifying. My life was laid bare - eating disorders, first heartbreaks, self harm, broken marriages and miscarriages - every page was a piece of my life, and my heart.
Her response blew me away,
"My dear Donna,
What powerful stuff you have written. Truly awesome! Tears, shock, many emotions - you have just made me go through all that! And I thank you. The really shocking stuff is I can relate to some of it - scary.
You should really be proud of yourself - they are really that good! Keep writing. If you wanted to have a look at publishing, maybe you might like to share with the www.?

Jen"

I'd never thought about sharing my poems before. Then suddenly it was all I could think about.

If my friend could relate to what I'd been through, then maybe so could others. Maybe it would make them realise they are not alone. We all face hurdles in life and it's ok to feel and fall. But hopefully they will also know they can fight.

At a very difficult stage in my life, my friend gave me new hope. She planted a seed of an idea that has stirred feelings in me again, given me that exciting butterfly flutter in my belly and made me question, could I?

ACKNOWLEDGEMENTS

My friends and family for their support and faith in my abilities. For their proof reading, feedback and encouragement.

Melissa Yendle for letting me use your amazing photographs of Nan and Bella holding hands and the girl against the fence, you are truly talented and I feel privileged to have your photos in my book.

To Juliusz, Lisa and Jen for putting up with my constant emails and calls for help relating to editing and photo specifications.

Masha from 'Mark Ashley Photography' for the use of my siblings family portrait.

Kerrie Yeates for your patience and helping me transform my thoughts and ideas for the books images into a reality.

Finally to Anne and the team at Balboa Press : A division of Hay House for your support and guidance through the process of publishing my book. Your commitment to clients and professional knowledge is outstanding.

Thank You
xoxo

INTRODUCTION

I am a survivor. From a turbulent childhood to many other journeys that life takes us on, I have documented fragments of my life through various pieces of writing, especially poems. Read about what it feels like deep within during battling bulimia, living with self-harming tendencies and unfaithful husbands, but don't give up.

These poems help me find my true self and also inner peace......

YOU DON'T KNOW ME

You see my clothes, my hair,
My job and my car.
But not the broken heart, the memories,
Nor under my clothes, the scar.
You don't know me.

You hear me speak, hear me laugh,
My steps with purpose, strong and tall.
But not the dullness of my eyes, the lost spark,
Or heard my cries/screams, the silent 'help' that I call.
You don't know me.

You feel my warmth, my compassion,
My tenderness, my frozen skin a minor detail.
But not the shaking hands, the pounding heart,
Or my burning lungs, as they struggle to inhale.
You don't know me.

You know my name, my children,
My house, maybe my peers.
But not my passions, my dreams,
Or my deepest, darkest fears.
You don't know me.

Yet you judge me, discuss me,
Make opinions formed from theories sewn.
Stop, look deeper, talk, ask, seek within,
Then you can make opinions of your own.
You don't know me at all.

UNBREAKABLE

The sun goes down, the week ends again,
Another night and a few more drinks.
Tempers rise, anger flares, names called,
Silently away to bed I slink.

I hold my hands over my ears,
Squeeze my eyes closed tight.
Nothing helps to drown out the sounds,
The bangs, cries, as you both fight.

My heart, it pounds, through my chest,
My body trembles, as I listen in fear.
To run out, shout, "STOP!","NO MORE!"
I cannot, I cower, lay frozen, shed a tear.

The damage observed, broken glass, maybe bruises,
As the sun rises, on yet another day.
The routines continue, as the norm,
But in silence, no words are there, to say.

Years go by, the cycle remains,
Through time links in the chain, rust, cracks appear.
History repeats itself, through generations,
Love, trust, hope, they disappear.

Through the despair and the dark depth of their broken souls,
The blood bond remains true and intact.
Demons are fought, strength found
And forgiveness given with arms tightly wrapped.

MY FIRST LOVE

My first love, my fairytale, I believed forever,
At sixteen years of age.
You, older, experienced, entered my life
At a puzzled and confusing stage.

I followed your lead, believed,
I was innocent and impressionable.
My downfall, demise, withdrawal
You were responsible.

You influenced all aspects of my life,
Where I went, what I did, even the clothes I wore.
You reeled me in, pushed me away,
Cheated, loved, and made me feel things I'd never felt before.

You held me down, whispered promises,
Betrayed me, forced your way in.
Continuously you, belittled and manipulated,
To make me believe, I'd committed a sin.

Down and desperate to keep you in my life,
I experienced bulimia, was force-fed through a drip.
And many scars were formed, both visible and within
My life, as it did a flip.

Everything changed that year,
My whole world turned upside down.
I lost friends, ran away from home,
And gained life long lessons with a permanent frown.

You ruined me, my future,
Forever filled with self-doubt and fears.
For a future with anyone else, will only ever be,
Of suspicion, worry, defenses and many shed tears.

3

THE HIDDEN ME

Freely flows the river of tears,
My heart races too fast.
My body shakes, I have no control,
Please don't let it last.

Breathing in or out is not an option,
The hand tightens its squeeze around my chest.
To regain myself, I have no other choice,
To old ways, I resort, to put the tornado within at rest.

It's never meant to be to die,
But just a slow release.
From the pain, pressure and confusion inside,
To be somewhat... for a moment... at peace.

I do not feel it as I cut,
Or the warmth of it's flow.
I only see it as it runs
And feel time, as it goes slow.

My breathing once more is calm and quiet,
And my heart beat no longer flies.
My body is not shaking, but aching,
And salt crystals form at the corners of my eyes.

And I sigh.

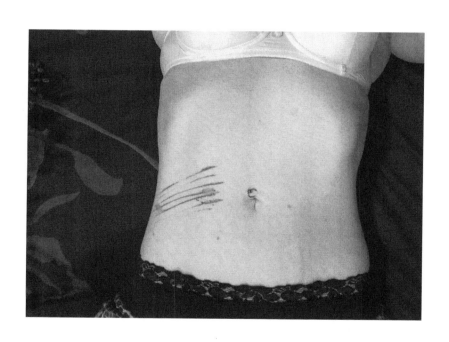

TO LOSE, IS TO WIN

"Ones struggle with bulimia and social pressures."

How I want you, love you
Too much at times it's true.
I need you, but must not have you
Eliminate you is the best thing to do.

You disgust me, repulse me
Make me feel ill.
If I indulge, even a little
I swallow a pill.

You must not stay
Get out ... leave quick.
If pills don't work
I'll make myself sick.

Nobody understands
This is my duty.
I can't change my thoughts
And was born no beauty.

"Plain Jane." "Nothing special."
"No hope, it's genetic."
Give up, it's no use
Just face it, I'm pathetic

DAD

A true gentleman, my hero,
My knight in shinning armor.
The only man a girl can ever trust,
My heart, my soul, my father.

From infant, toddler to teenager, we survived,
All grown up now, some might say, into a lady.
A special bond we hold you and I,
As I'll always be your baby.

From you I've learnt many things,
To build, garden, cook and more.
From you I get my passions/desires,
To do, push my self, envisage and explore.

You have your faults, made some mistakes,
Struggled and fought your demons within.
For this you are a role model,
A person to look up to and believe in.

You've held my hand in good times and in bad,
Been at my side at my very worst.
Your love and strength have held me together,
When you shed tears for me, my heart burst.

I thank you for your unconditional love,
Your devotion and for being you.
My love for you will never falter,
As I love you so, also, too.

MUM

Mum, you gave me life,
A sister and a brother.
You're a great wife,
And a wonderful mother.

I know, it's not been easy,
We've had our ups and our downs.
You've watched me grow from nappies,
To uniforms and graduation gowns.

I'm sure I've made you laugh,
Be angry, proud and cry.
Silly, serious or sad,
With you, I am not shy.

Your unconditional love,
Shines brighter than the sun.
For support and warmth,
It's into your arms that I run.

You've lifted me up,
When I was down.
Held me tight,
When I felt I'd drown.

You've held my hand,
Helped fight my fears.
Pushed back my hair,
And wiped away my tears.

You've shown me strength,
When I felt all was lost.
Stood up for me, protected,
No matter what the cost.

You and I, we're
Not just a well formed sum.
Friendship and loyalty,
I'm so proud to call you my Mum.

BROTHER

Farts, cubbies, rolling in the dirt,
in my hand a wooden gun.
BMX tracks with jumps, dips and turns,
Oh, big brother, we had fun.

You gave me many bruises, cuts,
bribes and girly tears.
But all was forgotten quickly,
As beside you, I had no fears.

From big bullies on buses
with bags swinging round.
To reassurance and whispers
on night time scary sounds.

At different ages and stages,
I thought you an alien from one planet or another?
A friend, a teacher, once even a stranger,
But always, my one and only, brother.

These days although we are hours away,
And miles keep us apart.
You are daily on my mind,
And forever in my heart.

SISTER

Lines were drawn across the room,
"Don't cross to my side" you would say.
Who would have thought after years gone by,
Best friends these two would be one day.

I was always messy,
You always neat.
To you a great big pain,
But i could also be sweet.

Over time we lived,
Through various ages and stages.
At least Mum and Dad
Didn't lock you in cages.

From zig zaggy fringe cuts,
Touch your make up I did not dare.
To hand me down dresses,
At least sometimes we could share.

To Sambucca shots,
And broken toilet seats.
Shared tears and fears,
And men - the cheats.

Now, jobs and cars, mortgages
And bills galore.
School, sports and play dates,
With our children, that we adore.

Although hours away,
And miles keep us apart.
You are daily on my mind,
And forever in my heart.

We survived, are alive,
Through the other side.
This day to day roller coaster called life,
We continue side by side.

With hugs and kisses,
Love, your little blister.

WHY?

For months you courted
Competed, clearly a win.
Then my heart you crumple, screw up
Discard in the bin.

Years have passed and I still question
My hat I take off and bowl.
How easily you walked away
From our wedded vow.

I left my family, friends
My life, for you.
All my hopes, dreams and
Forever, I said 'I do'.

For better or worse
In sickness and in health.
Till death do us part
Not, to rip out my heart.

We'd talk for hours
Till the sun went down.
You'd romance me, serenade
Make a smile from my frown.

One day you were here
Our dreams, future mapped out.
The next you were gone
Not a word, not a shout.

Was I not pretty enough?
Too fat? or too thin?
I'd have cut my hair,
I'm sorry for the colour of my skin.

What did she offer
That I could not give?
The two of you together, betrayed me
Stole my want to live.

DRAWN

Synthetic twines
braided together
swinging from the creaky beams.
Is it strong? too long?
Will it hold?

Drawn like a bee to nector.

Towels, tape and pipe
to buy
will trap the fumes within.
Gasp and choke?
Or drift to sleep?

Drawn like an addict to ice.

Gleaming metal
clean and sharp
glides through tender flesh.
Fast or slow?
Will I go deep enough?

Drawn like an alcoholic to liquor.

Winding road
along the cliffs edge
just a little veer to the right.
Fire? explosion?
Would I be identified?

Drawn like a gambler to money.

That tall tower
or a large bridge over water
to float free like a bird.
Scream or silence?
Who would find me?

Drawn like a Mosquito to blood.

Glistening cylinder
slides into place
squeezing tight the trigger.
Loud? Pain?
Who will clean the mess?

Drawn like tides to the moon.

Rainbow colors
small, round and smooth
my magic cocktail awaits.
Swallow, Drink, Swallow, Drink
Have I taken enough?

Drawn like me to you.

THE PLAYER

You're a chameleon
Of the night.
Broken hearted women
You set in your sight.

You take advantage
Of their vulnerability.
You charm, flatter
Ooze, your fake sensitivity.

With hope .. and stupidly trust
They take your hand.
Your intentions never more
Than a one night stand.

You fulfill your needs
Get your pleasure.
Oblivious to the damage done
The impact, you can not measure.

The space you warmed
Is empty by dawn.
Their hopes, self worth
Once again, broken and torn.

You strut, head held high
Stride on, it's another day.
They stop, smile, anticipate your approach
Without a pause, you walk on and turn away.

The thrill of the chase
Is all you were after.
Another notch on your belt
A story for the boys, with laughter.

BB3

Today ... August 23rd,
The day you were meant to arrive.
On Monday March 4th it was - much too early,
With no chance for you to survive.

I have shed so many tears for you,
They fall freely down my cheeks.
As life continues on each day,
It's been, minutes, days, now weeks.

Like yesterday, I remember,
So vivid and so, so detailed.
How you arrived so still and silent,
And of all the questions and of how I failed.

Your beautiful face, I still see,
So pale, as white as snow.
The sparkle of your eye, or their color,
Something, I will never know.

For the sun on your face, the wind in your hair,
Or for the breath, you will never take.
To the castles in the sand, the mud pies,
The silly jokes and funny faces you will never make.

The size of your hand, so tiny,
Eyes closed, so at peace.
Yet the impact on my heart so deep,
The pain, lose and memories I cannot release.

With support from family and friends,
And time, I know, our hearts will one day mend.
But our memories, dreams and love for you,
Will never, never, end.

NAN

Another Angel arrived in heaven today,
Free and at peace like a dove.
Behind she leaves family, friends and memories,
But most importantly her love.

Our hearts are broken and tears they fall,
But with time and memories, we will mend.
Our strong, determined Nan, already missed,
Back to Grandpa with love, we send.

There he stands patiently as he waits,
His arms open wide, a smile on his face.
Finally the two of you together again,
Your arms entangled in a longing embrace.

I can see you there, pain free at last,
A chuckle can be heard.
You are surrounded by those you have dearly missed,
To have kept you here, would have been absurd.

A lamington beside you, a cuppa in hand,
No shakes are there, in the kitchen in the sky.
You leave us here, yet return to many,
And for this, we will smile as we sadly bid you goodbye.

LOVE ME, LOVE ME NOT

To be alone
With hopes and possibilities.
Or to be with
But still alone.

You want me
But ignore me.
To be for another
Never will I be.

I stand always beside you
But am invisible.
I speak
But am not heard.

You real me in with promises
Yet discard them with every ale.
Beside you
I fade, I pale.

You show me no love
The flame within your fire, gone out.
Please ignite us once more
Or set me free, let go, I shout.

Into the shadows
I patiently wait.
For you to once again want
But will it be too late?

BB3'S 1ˢᵀ BIRTHDAY

Happy first Birthday,
My Angel in the sky.
I wish so much,
That you didn't have to fly.

It's been a whole year,
Since I said to you …"Goodbye."
I still remember like yesterday,
And my tears, are yet to run dry.

Sometimes I wish I knew,
One way or another.
Were you a sister for Kalani?
Or for Oscar, a little brother?

To see you in my mind so clearly,
It seems so wrong to not have given you a name.
Either way, our precious one,
Our lives will never be the same.

I hope you know how much you're loved,
You'll always be in our heart.
Our broken wing, our stolen angel,
Oh, how we were ripped apart.

Each year, this day is always yours,
I will, for you, try to be strong.
We will live, laugh, love and grow old,
But without you, it will always feel wrong.

MY PROMISE

Made to you dear Dad. At sixteen

Years of age.

"Please never hurt yourself again." from beside my hospital bed you plead,

Red eyes, fists curled, your shrunken frame I noticed, I nodded and agreed.

Over the years, it's been so hard.

Many obstacles in life have tested our pact.

I hold our bond very close to my heart. My promise to

Survive at every cost.

Every year that passes, for you, I've lived and not lost.

THE SPARK THAT NO LONGER FIRES

Love has needs
Just as lungs
Air it requires.
My body
Your touch
These are my desires.

One look, a caress
Sends tingles
My flame you ignite.
Hot breath, moist lips
Sweet moans
Only we, can unite.

Electric current
Internal quake
Shudders head to toe.
Tense, Arched
Grip tightens
Don't ever want to let go.

Time lapses
Memories distant
Thoughts, they give shivers.
Doubts, Fears
Questions?
Then tears ... quivers.

Please don't
Forget us
Don't shut me out.
Silent tears
"I LOVE YOU"
If only they could shout.

FORGIVENESS

For all the hurt and pain you have caused.

Over my body, patches of blue fade to yellow.

Remain in my memory forever they will, never to be forgotten.

Generated from anger, frustration or fear and fueled with substance. Yet still

I remain your loving, devoted wife. My wedding

Vows I promised and will take to the grave.

Everyday fragile and in fear of a repeat.

Never should've my children and I endured.

Every night I lay my head beside yours.

Sad, alone and with trepidation. It's only as you

Sleep, that I feel safe.

LONELY

Lost in my own thoughts,

Over and over they play.

Not able to see a way out,

Evaluate and analyze each day.

Love a far away memory,

Yearning my lost dreams of forever.

MY FRIEND

We've laughed, smiled and shared so many memories,
Over years, our friendship has held strong.
I cherish every minute/second we've shared,
Nothing will ever break our bond.

We've cried, yelled and held each other's hand,
Supported through all life's ups and downs.
Together we shared our hopes and our dreams,
Encouraged, reassured, made smiles from frowns.

We are family chosen, not by blood,
I believe in you and am here by your side.
My pride for you and all you've achieved,
I will show you, praise and not hide.

We see each other as we are,
Accept, no pretending, acts or disguise.
Our thoughts, feelings, deepest secrets,
With you, I never have to improvise.

We've seen one another at our best and our worst,
And still our friendship effortless, together, we remain.
A true friend found, so rarely, I value our unconditional love,
To cherish, treasure and nurture us - I will promise to maintain.

They say if you've been friends for more than seven years,
Your friendship will last forever.
How lucky am I to have you in my life,
In the past, now and into the future, together.

LOST

You've broken my heart,
Killed my self-esteem.
Walked out our families door,
Throwing away our dreams.

A new life you've formed,
One without me, I no longer share.
I sit in bewilderment, fear and uncertainty,
It's so unfair.

For six years I've sat and waited,
For you to be the father I've always seen you could be.
Now, as you share days and experiences with them,
I'm saddened, why now? Why not with me?

An open book you asked me to hold,
Keep open, for you to change your mind.
Each day goes by, more pain, lies and hurt,
Pages turn, the end near, you'll soon be left behind.

Not short enough or thin,
Not what you'd pictured your future to be.
I am what you fell in love with, the same,
Open your eyes, look, and you will see.

Wife, Mother, I couldn't have done more,
100% devoted, forever, to you.
But it still wasn't enough, you're not happy,
What else could I possibly do?

I stumble, trip through each day,
Some strong and some in despair.
I will get through this, I know, be stronger,
No longer submissive, please beware.

You can't expect me to wait,
Sit idle, why you play around.
My happiness, joy and laughter, my goal,
To once again be found.

MY LIFE

You are the light at the end of my tunnel,
You have been my saviors from despair.
My heart, my soul, my true loves forever,
My clean, fresh breath of air.

When days are dark, you make them bright,
My frown, you always turn to a smile.
If things seem hard, you make them easy,
Every second spent with you, is worthwhile.

Your innocence, your spark for life,
Shines brighter than stars in the night sky.
Your characters, your energy,
Endless, never runs dry.

I watch you grow, learn and change,
I often at night, watch you sleep.
Your hand I hold, your cheeks I kiss,
Your tears I wipe when you weep.

My favourite sound to hear, are your giggles,
My favourite feeling, the touch of your hand.
Years of ups, downs, doubts and confusions,
Through you, my reason for life, I have found.

I cannot promise you life's going to be easy,
I cannot promise I won't make mistakes.
I can promise you I'll try my hardest, love you forever,
And I can promise you I'll do whatever it takes.

You are my life, my dreams,
You are my children.

FIGHT ON

For the future, my children, family and friends,
I stay determined, strong and fight on.
Gather strength and knowledge through experiences, to
Help me through this journey, called life.
Tomorrow the sun will rise on another day,

Only I can write my futures goals.
Never in my text will it say 'I gave up.'

Another day, means another chance, a
New beginning and a fresh start.
Determined to forgive and forget the past,

Believe in, dream of what's to come, and
Enjoy and appreciate what is now.
Love, respect and help others
I vow to continue on.
Enjoy life, let go, live and laugh.
Value the simple things in life, a smile, a sunrise and
Every day that I am alive.

AGAIN

I've been hurt, broken and abused,
Dragged down and held under.
But I'm strong, determined, I won't give up,
Fight till the end, I will not surrender.

I hold on to hope, I cherish what I have,
Prey that I can let go of the past.
This is my journey, another phase,
Before me a shadow I must not cast.

Hold strong to me, what I truly believe,
Live, Laugh and Love like there's no tomorrow.
Stand tall, Dream big, protect those close to me,
Eventually, I will bury this sorrow.

From the dark depths of my broken heart,
Once again butterflies will flutter and be felt.
With a touch of a hand or a simple smile,
The past tension and pain will freely melt.

This is me, this is who I am,
Broken soul, scars and a history.
Love me all, as I am, accept and believe in me,
The future ? ..... well, it's a mystery.

Printed in the United States
By Bookmasters